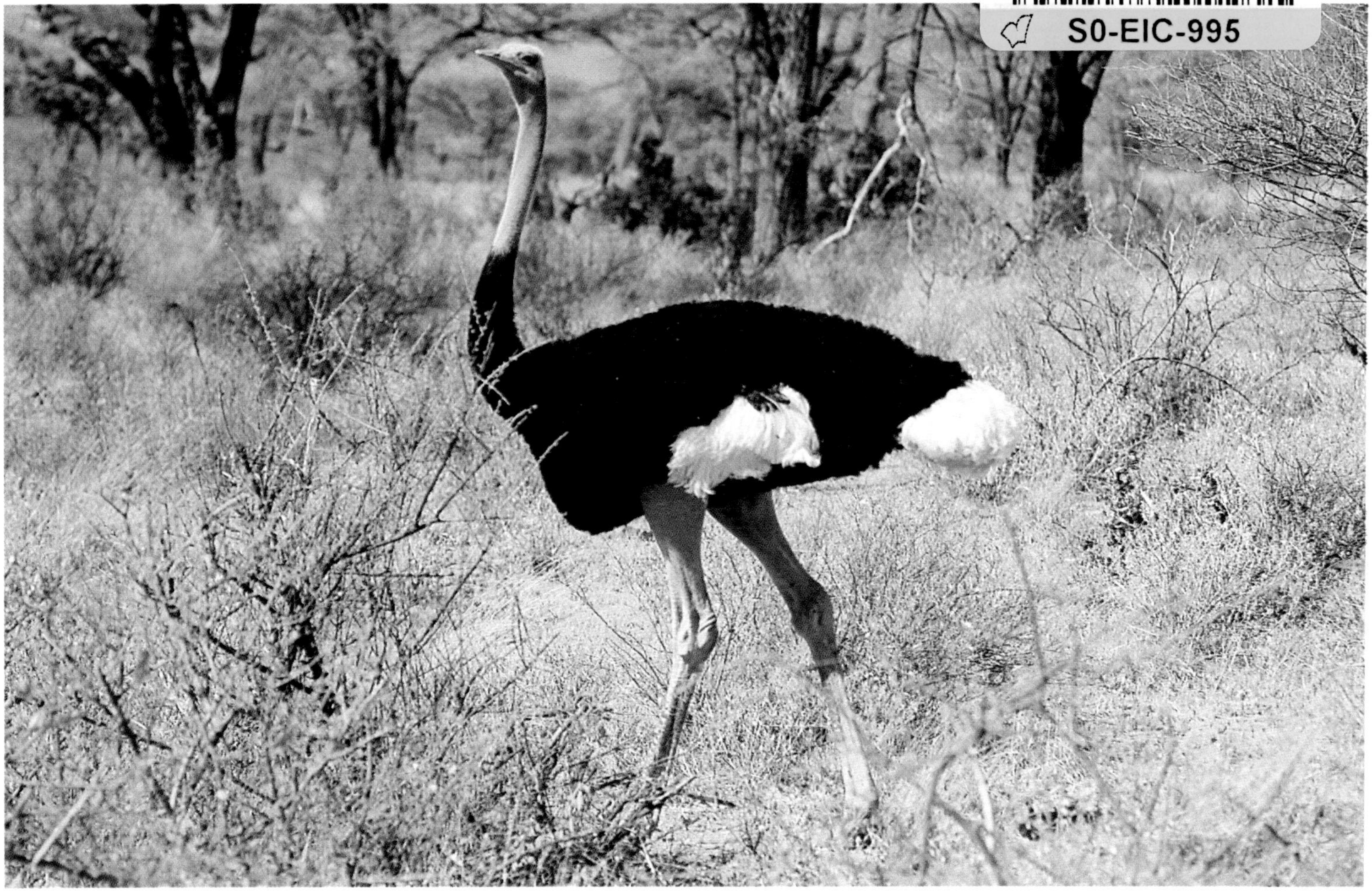

ostrich

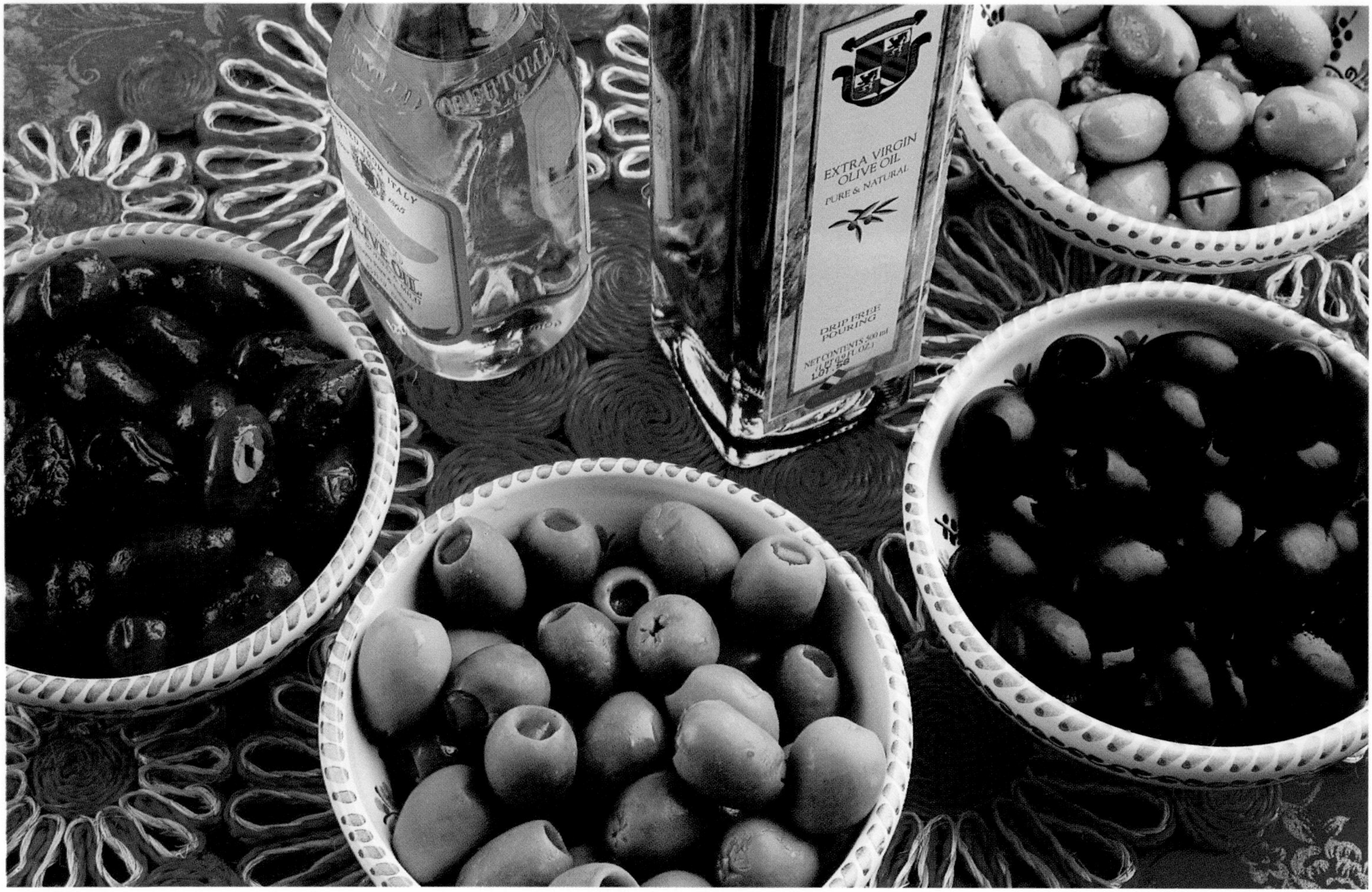

olives

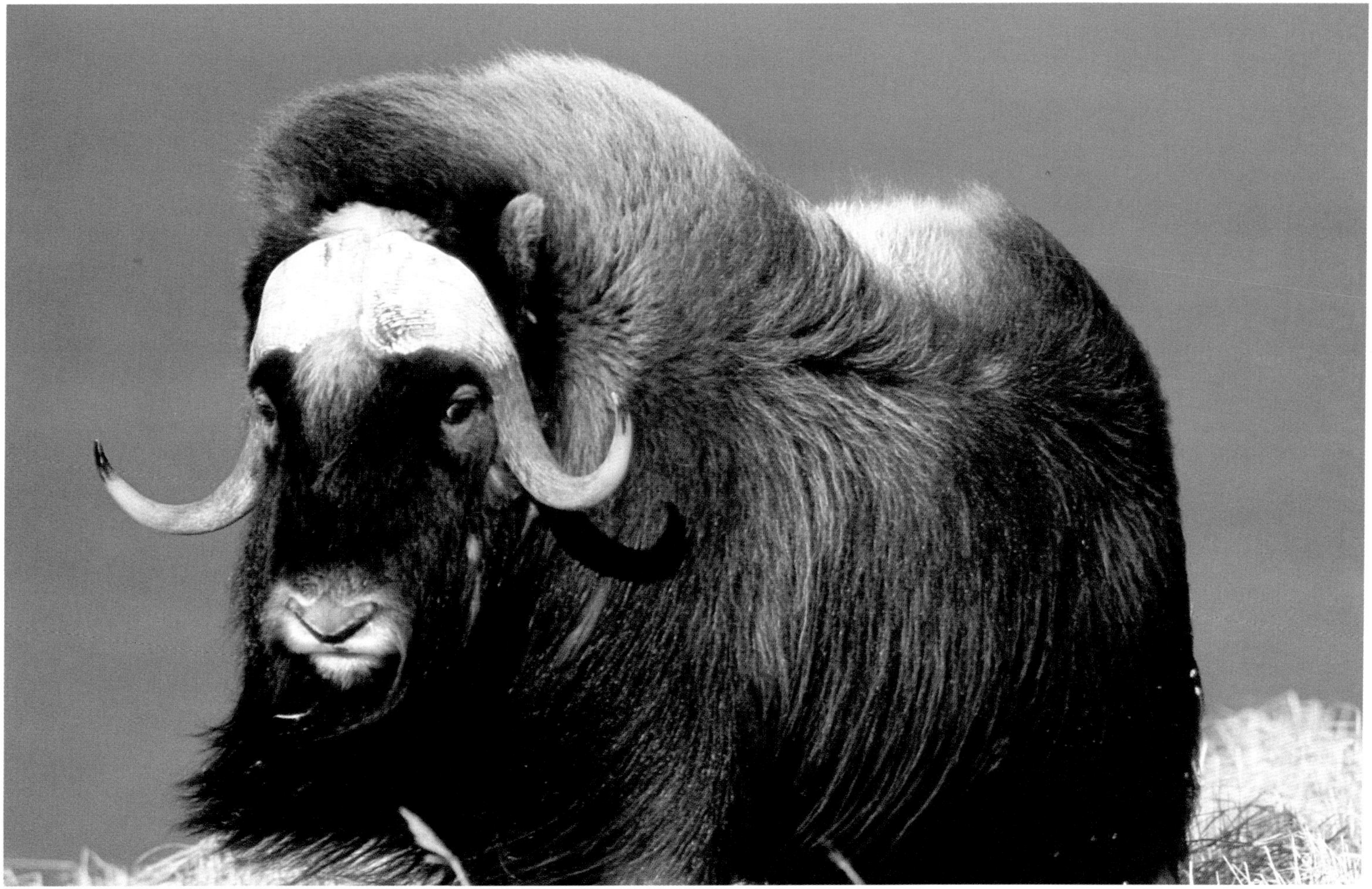

OX

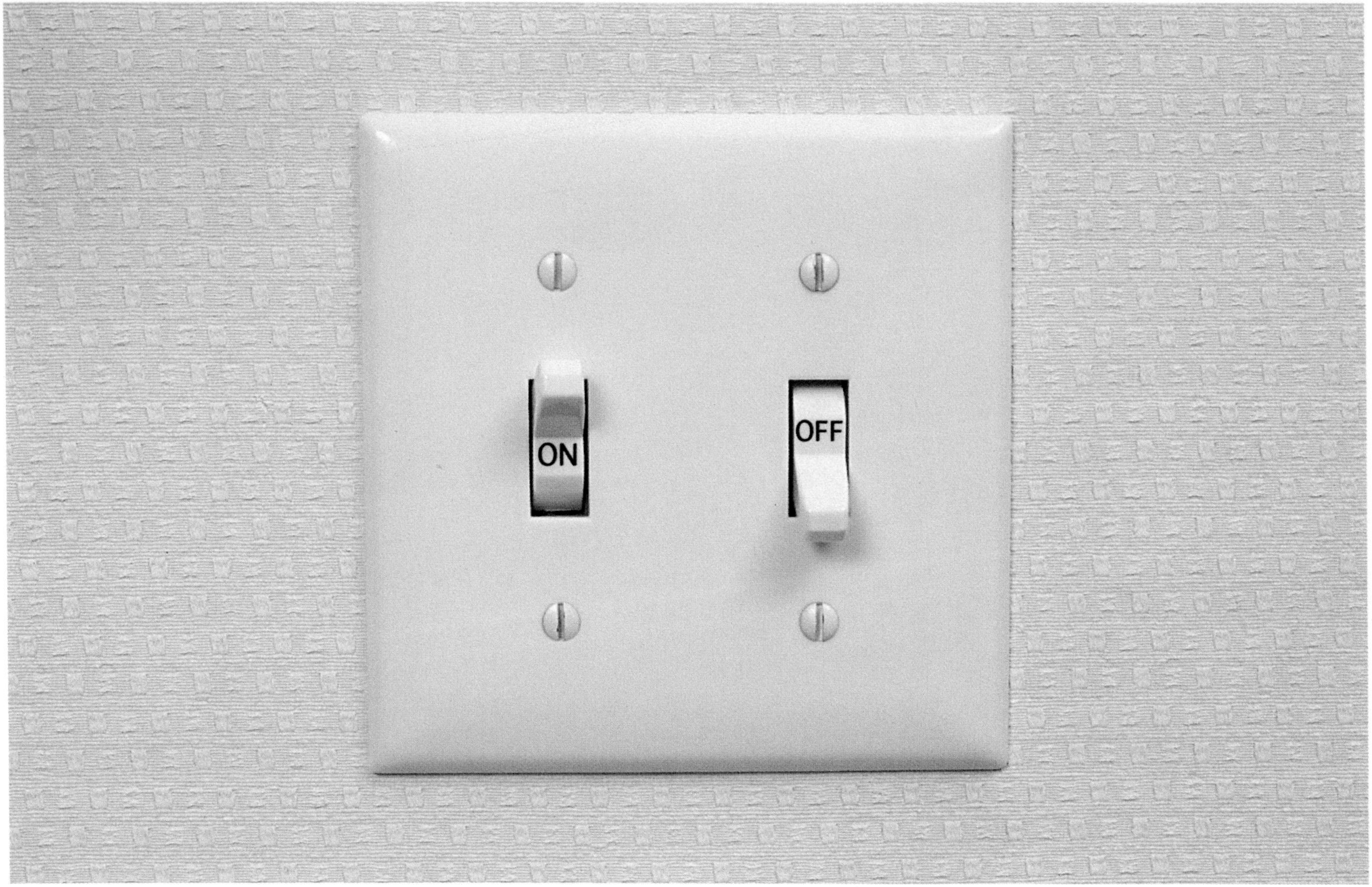

on off

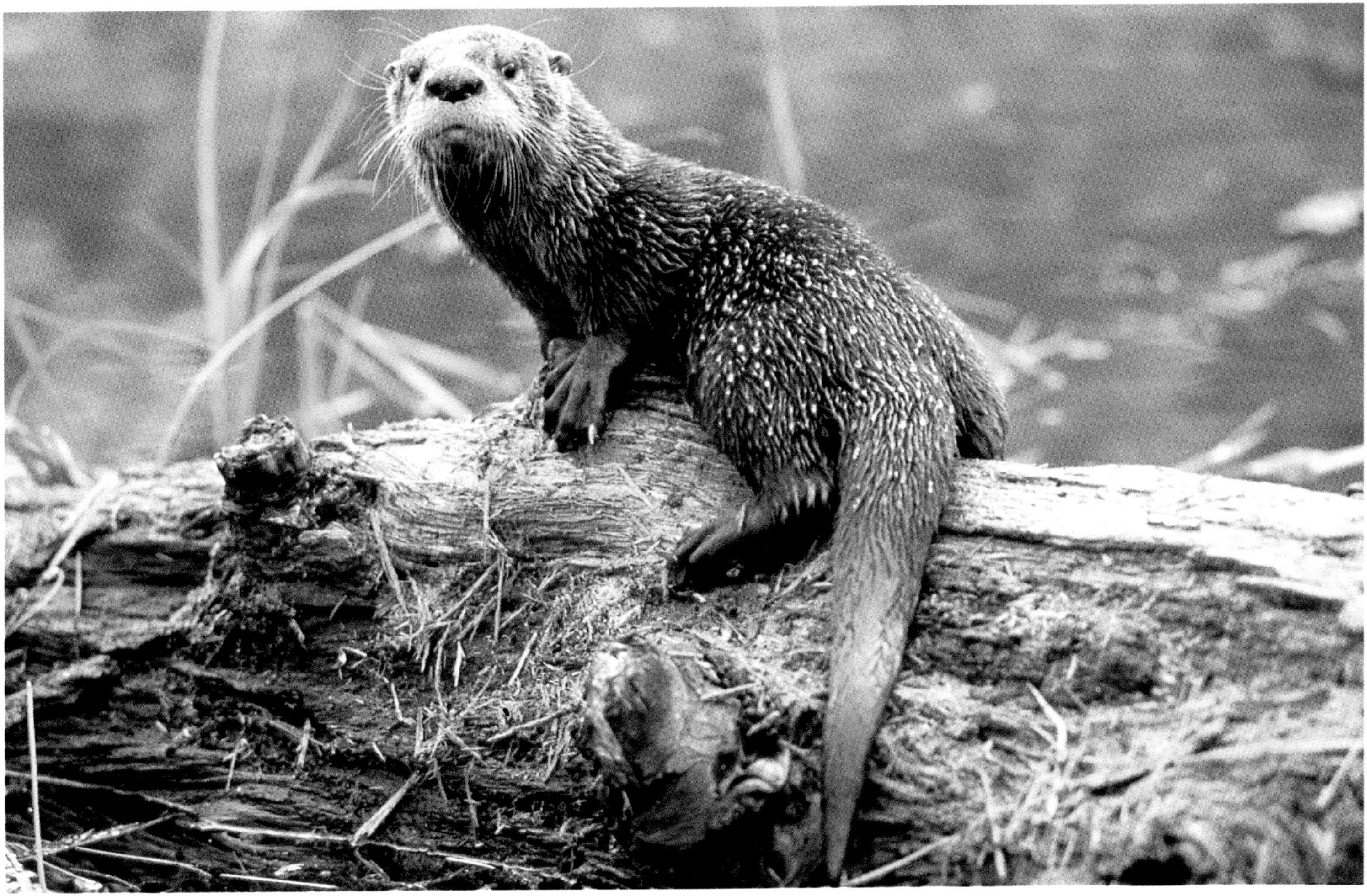

otter

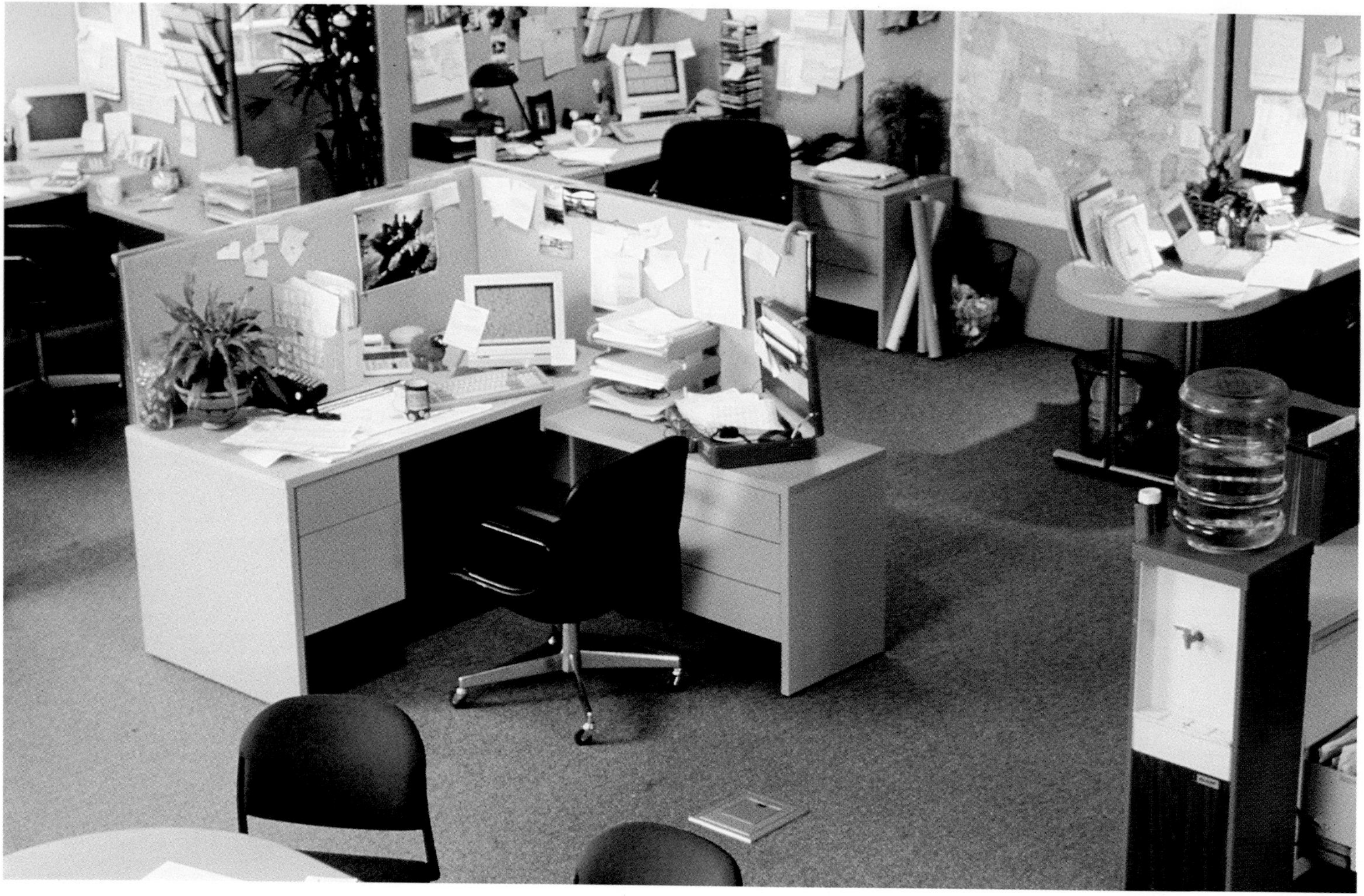

office

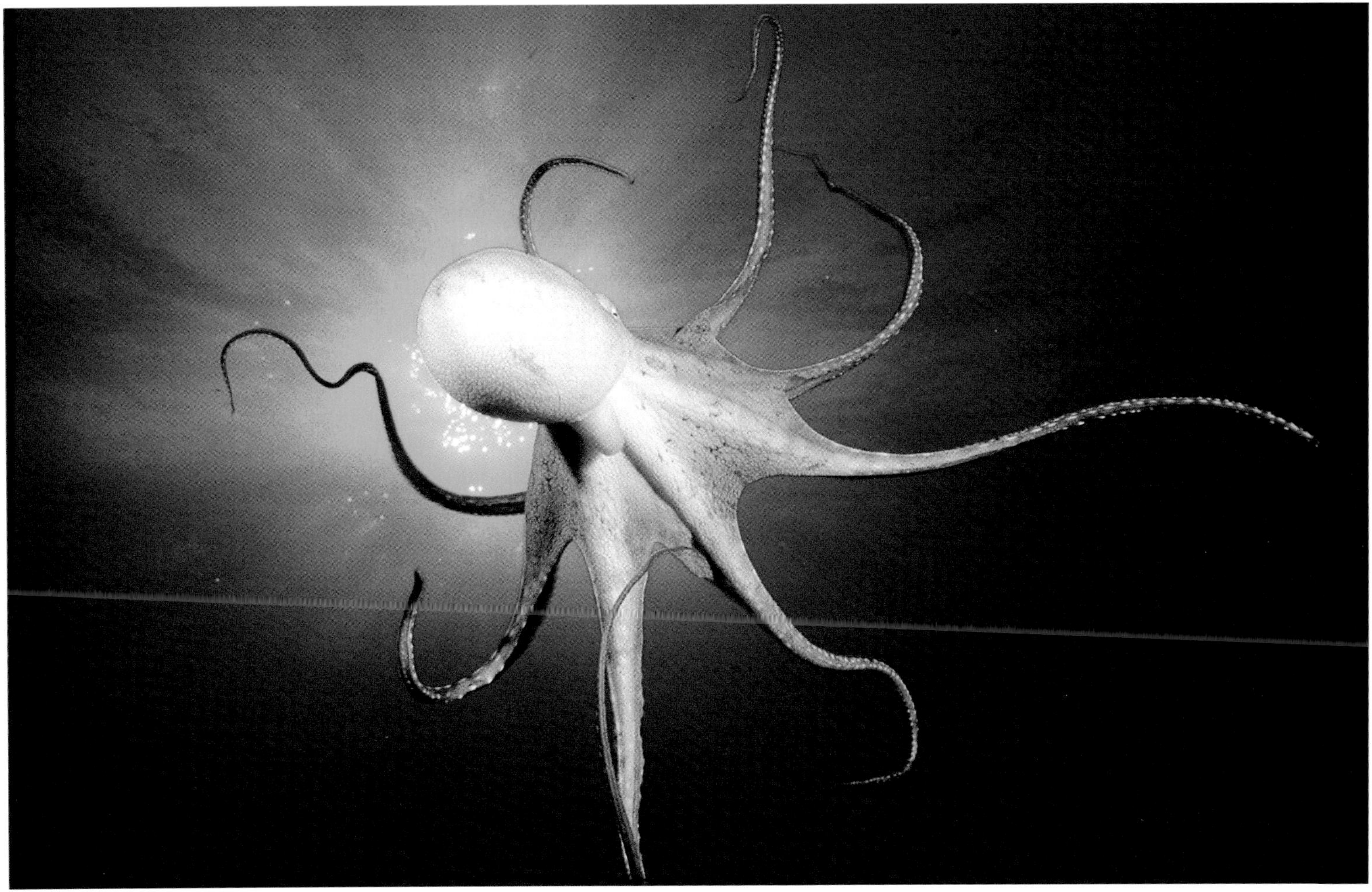

octopus

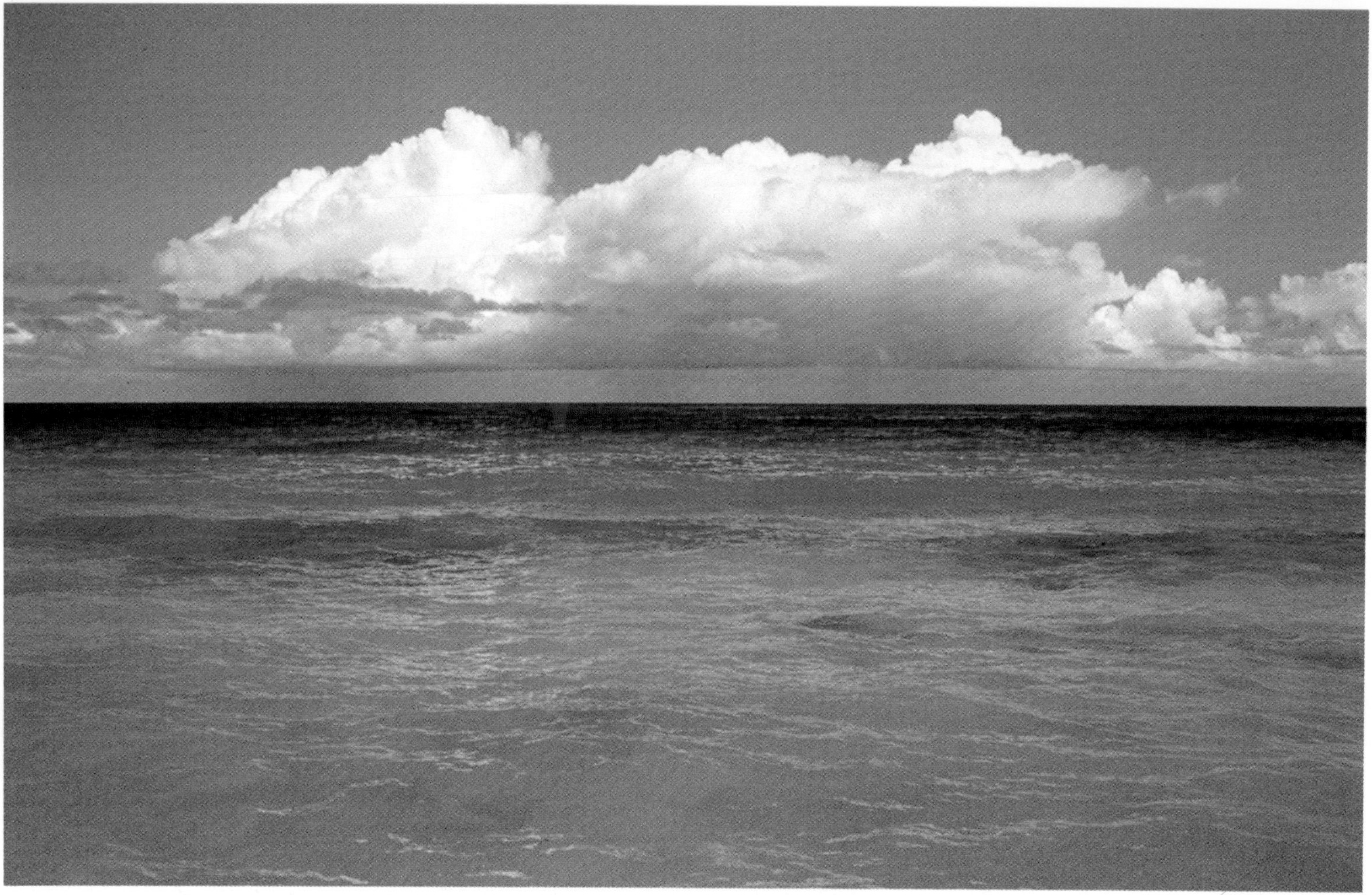

ocean